Love is Not a F♥cking Swear Word

Stef Mann

Dedicated to Harvest.

ISBN: 9781700078353

Contents

❤

♥

Disclaimer

I'm going to be flat out honest with you, I don't care if you agree with what I say in this book and I want you to take that to heart. I mean that because this is a book about love. It's about opening the door to a new possibility and ultimately helping you access more love. And... there's more than one recipe to get us there.

Maybe you feel like you have the whole love thing locked down and perfected. However, the funny thing about love, it's not something you can have too much of, so what is there to lose?

What I do care about is the something I also tell my clients all the time: I don't expect you to have a cookie cutter version of my beliefs. That is: I want you to just consider something different, even a split second. I'll admit it would be fabulous if you turn these pages and get an ah-ha moment that brings you or someone else you know a tiny bit closer to feeling more loved, less alone, and all around better about who they. I don't think anyone would say that we need less love and if they do, they're probably lying to themselves.

You do you. Only take from my book what you need and fill in your own gaps. I call that the 80/20 rule. Never take more than 80% of what someone says, because if you take more, you're just trying to be them and you're no longer leaving space for you to come in. That is my learning philosophy. There is never one "right" way to think or believe so I want you to take pieces that resonate with you and fit them into your life, your perception of reality.

I will tell you that I've sat on this book (not literally) for a while and I've made space for some pretty good thinking moments. Keep this book on hand, read it in pieces or all at once. Mark pages that resonate the most and share the snippets that drive an intellectual conversation whether it be in agreement or not. This is not a chance to be right or wrong, it's a chance to expand. When you work from a place of no judgements you only leave room for possibility and expansion. Judgement limits our scope.

Changing your mindset has huge impact on you and those around you. Dive right in and see if anything shifts. Thank you for considering a step in a direction that I believe could help people feel more loved and positive everyday. It means a lot and much love to you.

Xoxo, Stef

1
Why an Unconventional Love Book

I was raised in a very loving home. My mom would have done anything for us kids and still does to this day, and my dad has always been someone who strives to speak my language, no matter how much my perspective on life changed over time. I was fortunate enough to have such amazing love in my life from day one, but I've always been an incredibly sensitive person. I knew I had people who loved me, but my sensitive side had trouble taking in that love sometimes. It wasn't until I was in my mid-twenties was I actually able to work with that energy and combine the love and sensitivity into something that allowed me to accept the love, struggle less in my social interactions, and even just understand my place in the world.

When I was 15 years old, I met a boy who was one of my friend's cousins. For no other apparent reason than to just be a flat out jerk, he told me that I was a freak and that no one would ever love me or want to ever be with me. Excellent thing to say to a young teenage girl to boost her already damaged self-image, or not! Our teenage years are pivotal point in our lives and in mine I was already battling with mistrust of others and myself. It was only the middle of *years* of being bullied, teased, and almost always feeling like an outcast in social circles. Looking back, I'm actually thankful for every moment of it because it led me to exploring deeper into the many reasons to people act the way they do, understanding that love comes from within, and sparked my path of learning all the things that I have from self-acceptance to forgiveness of others. All of which have brought me more joy and less anxiety.

Later in life, I became a front row audience member to the most popular day that love is expressed in a public setting: weddings! As a wedding photographer for over ten years, I've seen the impact our society has on people when it comes time to see ourselves in photos. It's the time we get most critical about every little bit of ourselves we hate and want to change what we have been told is wrong. Almost every wedding client I have ended up talking with them about their feelings of self-love or self-loathe before even taking the pictures, which put me in a unique place of helping dozens of people overcome a few of their obstacles. I've also seen the variety in how couples outwardly express their love from the over-the-top, to comfortable couples, to platonic love between their closest friends. The complicated love of family that fuels chaos and calm, and the love of everyone involved to make the day happen. Even those who express love through their business as a service provider such as myself.

I've spent years doing the psychological, spiritual, and energetic work to unpack the impact those things have had on my life and that's why I now seek to help others ease the speed bumps of getting to a place where they can feel good about themselves and access more love. Armed with a thirst for knowledge and understanding of others, a variety of training and a whole lot of personal experience, my revelation has been that by accessing more love, we can overcome anything that holds us back. Even while writing this book, I've experienced my own ins and outs of what love is and how it is experienced and all it did was strengthen my views and expand the love I have even more, even in the face of adversity.

I believe knowledge is meant to be shared and I don't just mean the knowledge in textbooks and regurgitated on school exams. I mean the knowledge of experience. The knowledge of wonder. The knowledge of questioning all that you have been told before so that you can stand up and create your own belief systems. The knowledge of knowing you just want more. The knowledge of knowing that only you can hold your own truths.

That all starts with a different perspective on something you think you know all about. I wrote this to help you question and solidify what love means for you. Even if it just helps you know your own perspective a little more.

2
A Swear Word?

I remember when I was little and an adult who was twice my size and what seemed to be 20 times my age would throw out a swear word. Right in the middle of the sentence - gasp - someone said the F word! It was bad, it was a crime to an impressionable six-year-old and even my dad had to throw coins in a jar just for uttering such language.

As I got older and headed into my double digits of age, using these so called swear words began to see even bigger consequences. I remember when I was in grade 4 on the school playground and another child stole my POGS*. I was furious. My Lion King POGS that I had done endless chores in order to buy - stolen by some punk kid on the playground. Being a rather small child, I used the only tool I had: words. I shouted out to that kid and called her an asshole and demanded my POGS back. This action landed me in the principal's office, something that probably only happened once or twice in my stint in the educational system, and received the same punishment as the girl who stole from me. In our society at that time, swear words uttered by a child had a similar consequence to stealing and that's what my takeaway was.

In a more recent event, I met a child who was taught that these words were scary. So scary that an extended family member who uttered them was no longer one that could be trusted to be around the child, yet they had done nothing else wrong. Her parent had pestered the child to ask why this person was scary, asking if it was because of his swearing and so she had nothing else to go on other than feelings so that must be the reason why she was uncomfortable. She had learned that this ultimately was something incredibly bad, something that made the family member dangerous because of it. This small word led to increasing a family rift due to the mistrust created around these simple utterances. That is a huge impact! One that will impact the child and her family forever. Ouch.

We were taught that even though these words existed we couldn't use them. While I'm someone who now believes that these words are just that - words - and can be used as seen fit by the speaker, I often [try to] avoid using them around small children as respect for those who find offence in it. Offence like the child felt, or we all know what it would feel like to walk into a room full of people and drop an F-bomb into a crowd that doesn't welcome of it. Even the term "F-bomb" is so perfectly fitting, because that's the impact it has for some people: an explosive, shocking effect.

Why does this all matter in a book about love? This is what a swear word in our society is represented as: a shocking, take back word that we are scared to say due to consequences.

Yet we have a similar knee-jerk reaction to the word **love**.

I look back on my own experience and I notice how I've treated the word love like a swear word with all the strings attached. While I have an endless list of experiences both good and bad, the best one is probably the more relative to my current life.

When my now-husband first told me he loved me, it was a bit of an interesting experience. He took me out to dinner which was about a thirty-minute drive away, and the entire time he insulted me, thinking he was just joking around. The sensitive side of me took over and started to take offence to his jokes. If you know me, you know I'm someone who likes to joke around a lot but I was feeling hurt by all the remarks he was making especially as we were headed for a very fancy meal out.

We had only been dating for a couple months, and had really only been friends for about half a year. As we sat down to enjoy our meal, with my ego feeling a bit bruised from all his bashing, he held my hand and awkwardly spurted out some compliments, as if it would soften how the drive went. After a blur of words brushed by my head, he spurted out that he loved me.

He *loved* me. Excuse me?

You got it. I had that knee-jerk reaction of what the heck are you saying! Even though if I look back now I knew that I loved him in that moment as well, in the moment I felt part of a silly high school romantic comedy and I just awkwardly said "thanks!" I followed that with an honesty saying it's was too soon for me to reciprocate the words. I fell into that perception of all the things that seemingly come with the word love. It's how I was brought up in this culture and society.

Now you're probably wondering when I finally got the guts to say "I love you" back, since I'm writing a book about the topic of love. I wrote it to him on my phone about a week later. I wasn't quite so lame as to text it to him, but I had written "I love you" in the notes app on Christmas morning and since he was sleeping in the bed next to me, I stealthily slid it under his face when I realized he was about to wake up.

When he opened his eyes and saw the message,

he got super excited and even in that moment, it was hard for me to verbalize my emotions so I just awkwardly smiled back at him.

What did those three little words really mean? I knew I felt love, but what did it mean to actually say it to a romantic partner who I hadn't been dating as long as I thought I should.

In my experience, we are afraid to tell people we love them in fear of consequences. We are afraid what this word really means and all it encompasses. We have trouble saying it in fear of the strings it attaches. We hold so much value in that tiny four letter word alone, dependent on someone else, yet we fail to shower the value upon ourselves. We use the word as an all or nothing, an ultimatum and sometimes the lack of being able to say the word is a threat. We start wars because of love, people end their lives because of it and our lives are miserable without it being said to us.

Love is very powerful thing and what if instead of holding on to an "all or nothing" implication of the word, we were able to redefine it so that it can be even more widespread and effective? What if we no longer treated it like a four letter swear word? What would the impact be on the world? On you?

Take a moment to think about the word love and the initial reaction you have. Is it a positive one or does it seem to come with a sense of "shhh don't say that"? If it is a positive one, does it come with a bunch of strings attached or does it flow smoothly without conditions?

Let's work together to make the word "love" feel a little more normal or if it already does, to access more of it in your everyday life. Especially in the places you wouldn't normally think it to be.

For the joy of dating myself: POGS (or as Wikipedia defines more generically as a game called milk caps) was a childhood trading and playing game consisting of thin small round cardboard pictures and thicker game piece called a slammer. It helped bridge my obsession of enjoying any sort of trading and playing game, later moving into Magic: The Gathering and Pokemon cards.

3
Redefining Hollywood Love

Before we can think about how we redefine love so that it is no longer something we fear or lack, what is love to you? Write it down so we have a reference. Here you go, I even gave you some pretty space (thanks to the graphic designer inside me):

....

Love, to me is:_____

_____

....

Now that you have that down, let's talk about some concepts around what love is, and for argument sake, what it isn't.

I'm not talking about "Hollywood love," which is what most of us based our definition on or at least stem it from. Hollywood love is the head-over-heels for one person that you must spend your life with, have a mad passionate romance with every night, and check off your ideal person boxes with. Hollywood love is also the love you have for your offspring who you would do anything for and that others will never understand unless they are a parent. Hollywood love is what people would do anything for and if they don't have it - their life is incomplete, for how can they live without that love?

Thinking back to my own story of how I feared saying I love you to my now husband when he said it to me, I think I was waiting to see those crazy sparks of Hollywood before I could say it back. At the time, that whole picture-perfect package had to be there in order for it to be true!

To me, that's a little overwhelming. It's a lot of pressure wrapped up into one little word rather than expanding it into its positive potential and a more accessible point. Love is meant to be something that everyone experiences in their own way, and it's something that would be considered an essential ingredient for life. You got it: an essential ingredient for life, like oxygen and water.

So what is love? In this book, we'll explore some possibilities rather than just give a bunch of boring dictionary type definitions. If we simplify it too much, then we risk only focusing on what love isn't and we may misunderstand real love when it appears in our life. What if it's just everything, yet nothing in particular? It could be an array of magical things that we know provides nourishment to our lives and all the tiny vibrating cells that we and everything around us are made up of.

When we broaden and loosen our definition of love, it becomes easier to recognize and experience while still respecting we all have our different perceptions of reality and will alter how we feel, see and relate to things.

I'd like to start by jotting down what love is based on some of my personal experiences of this more open concept love is, rather than my previous stereotypical one to ensure that while it helps to put a placeholder on how vast it is, it is still vague enough to have your own interpretation fit in.

Love is a friend texting you just to say hi. Love is the tree reaching to the sky for light to grow. Love is a dog wagging its tail chasing a ball. Love is accepting that you are different and owning that. Love is taking this time to learn what it might be to you, playing out in a form of self-love. Love is learning to laugh in the face of fear for the thrill of where life wants to take you. Love is knowing you care about someone inclusive of the things you don't like. Love is an understanding of people who don't understand you and trying to bridge that gap. Love is appreciation for anything and everything. Love is a simple mutually beneficial energetic exchange. Love is like the universe, like spirit, like God (or whatever higher power you may resonate with), you believe it is all around you and you find it in everything, or you choose to believe it's not there because you can't see it. It's not something you turn on. You are attempting to turn on experience, one that you believe to be love. While love is there, it's just so much more inclusive and widespread.

Love is everything in an expression of joy. Joy is love. Once you feel that, once you embody that, you will see love everywhere. Choose love, and love chooses you because love always wins. Then you can start to manifest the expression of love you which to enhance – real connections with people, love with romance, love with intimacy, love with real conversation. Love becomes the base of everything you want to experience and already know is there, the rest comes after. Love can be found in everything, love is in you and you are love.

4
The Heart & Head

Are you following your heart? It's one of the things we are taught, especially when moving into alignment with intuition and living a life of what we actually want and need. That phrase is something we grew up with when we are seeking relationships, following our dreams or even just making big life changes. When we follow our hearts and we'll more likely get what we want most. For a book that aims to find love in the places we may not have looked before, you would think it would all be about only working from your heart space and leaving your head behind, when in fact, it's actually about working with both. As you read through the context of each chapter, a lot is to do with thinking things through, while finding that warm and fuzzy side which involves your heart.

When I first started to work more from my heart rather than my head and understood that love is something that is found everywhere and in everything, it actually dissolved some of my practical life skills that were important.

An example that comes to mind is I have a long-time friend and we've built up each other in our lives, career, and overall capacity to become better humans. Many times throughout our relationship I chose to lead everything from my heart, I knew the feeling that we needed to help each other through our journeys and that we both had a good impact on each other's lives. While many of our conversations were intellectually stimulating, we had a few disagreements over time and because of that there were feelings that got hurt.

Coming from a place where I always wanted to forgive and that is what my heart was telling me, I found love in our relationship that kept me going but I forgot to include my rational thoughts of boundaries when they were needed. This is very typical of many people who live with "love wins"-based mentalities, constantly choosing to forgive and let the practicality fall away when they actually need to put some thought into the situation. This relationship ended up backfiring because I didn't use my head to think out how it was playing out and the dynamic was thrown off and we ended up having to put a pause on the friendship. Something that may have been avoided if I coupled my heart-based actions with some more rational thought.

We eventually did find each other again and now I consciously work from my heart with the strength of my thoughts so there is always an open, loving, feeling with boundaries on both sides. I chose love.

I wanted to add this concept of following your head in a book of love because when you follow a new pattern of what love is and look for it in the places that you may not have found it before, it actually requires a bit of thought. You need to use your head to implement new concepts. Mindset requires thought and so does general understanding of new ideas and discovery.

If we were to function solely from the heart, we fall back into our previous interpretation of love. When we follow our heart, it's all about the feelings involved, and a lesson learned countless times from a couple of impactful people in my life.* Feelings are subjective and they change. They aren't facts or even opinions.

Feelings are just emotions that are charged up in a moment. Most of us, myself included, experience pretty dramatic feelings when we're hungry or tired. We revert back to a five-year-old having a tantrum and that's not really reliable, is it? We make it only about the desires we crave and while it's sometimes based on intuition or even situationally based, it might be leading us down a path that we'll have to circle back around to. The love that we follow just from the heart may be part illusion, a mask that hides all the extras, or just the fact we need to eat something!

If we only functioned from the heart, we'd start careers without even thinking about what skills we really need to be successful in that career. We'd jump into relationships that just make us just feel good instead of actually fulfilling all the bits and pieces we need to make it work. So, as we look for opportunities that are full of love or looking for more love to connect to, we need to think about it as well, not just feel it. A simple check-in with yourself mentally without overthinking things will suffice.

To give some examples of working with both, let's go with some common ways that are beneficial to find love and use your heart and your head:

Meeting the person of your dreams and making sure they aren't a serial killer.

Going after the career that speaks to you but first getting the experience or education needed to do it.

Working on a charity project but making sure it will actually make a difference in the world you want to live in.

Doing kind things for others but with setting your own boundaries.

Discovering the spiritual world without losing your grounding in this reality.

Asking yourself if you are in integrity with yourself while weighing the options of self-love vs selfish love.

What is something you "followed your heart on" and could have used a little brain power with?

....

I followed my heart _____ and could

have used my head for _____.

....

We may be working from a place of love, finding love, and experiencing more love which in turn connects us to our hearts, which is a beautiful place to live in. However we can't forget to bring those brains in as well. To simplify: you need your heart as well as your head to experience, spread, and understand more love.

Shoutout to Brian & James.

5

Love & Loss

As I had started to write this chapter, my two-year-old dog Harvest was fighting for her life in a very blind-sighted illness. While it may be a weird time to think about writing about love, like all the things we learn in life, it is actually synchronistically perfect.

I found myself in that moment of desperation of trying to find an answer about Harvest's health challenges, trying to do everything possible to make the situation better. Sometimes in those situations all you can do is leave space for things that you didn't expect. The beauty in the way the universe functions is that we are often faced with challenges so that we are given the opportunity to value what is there. When you are most scared of losing someone you love, you have hope and knowing there is more to their story that plays out in your own life.

When we're in a state of losing love, whether it be a loved one or even the loss of a relationship, many times we react by vowing to never want to love in that way again. It hurts to lose that warm feeling of a connection in one way or another so why would we ever want to lose it again?

Operating on a wavelength of loss as a complete negative isn't helpful to anyone though, especially yourself. If we view love in a way that we can just lose it, will we ever fully embrace it? However, if we view love as something that is ever growing, something that is always there and never gone, we can look at loss as just loss of the connection, loss of the companionship, loss of the humour that connection brought you. The love is never lost and if we choose to see it as just a change in the relationship, then we can stop feeling like we can lose love. If we stop feeling like we can lose it, then we can automatically be more open to seeking it, keeping it, not being afraid of it and embracing it – full on.

While you may lose a loved one who passes away or even walks away, you still have the love that you built in that time together. Memories and feelings of happiness don't simply disappear. The love you felt inside of you may feel gone but it never really disappears because it is YOU who has loved and you don't simply stop loving as you are still existing. You may lose someone who makes you laugh – but does your ability to laugh stop? You may lose something that makes you feel safe, but isn't it you who decided that it was what made you safe in the first place? Isn't it possible that you can decide to feel safe again?

Those are just the things connected to the love, not love itself.

If you find yourself losing something or someone that maybe was deliberate such as a relationship ending, it isn't love you are now losing. You still built love for yourself, love for new things and even a connection of love between each other. That energy may still be there but it may morph into something different, such as love for yourself that you were able to grow while still letting go.

I find this particularly relevant when it comes to relationships ending as per choice of both people involved. I can remember a man I once dated and I thought he was the one that I was going to spend my life with. I loved him dearly and he was very special to me. When it came down to the time where we decided the relationship had to end and we needed to go our separate ways, it hurt. It was a huge loss in both our lives at the time. We both had empathy for what each other needed and we realized that it couldn't happen by staying together. I even remember saying to him a few days before we split up that he had the choice of providing me with what I needed, or we would break up. Even by asking that very question, I knew we had to part our ways because I was no longer truly loving him for who he was in that moment.

After asking that question, I knew my love for him had to change into something different: a love for respecting what we both needed and wasn't being fulfilled in our relationship. Eventually our love turned into friendship, but we slowly drifted apart. Even to this day, I see that love in other forms – in respect for myself in what I need, in the path those choices led me to, and all the things that he taught me being together and the memories we shared. Most of all, he was a stepping stone to knowing what I needed in the guy I did marry. That loss has never taken away the love.

This also comes into play when relationships unexpectedly end or when it's a relationship that you feel like you would have been better off without even having at all. Another guy I dated, appeared to be everything I thought I was looking for at the time - cute, strong, a rule-breaker, drummer. He'd always tell me I was pretty (what every girl longs to hear from a partner). But when it came down to it, he was actually a pretty crappy person overall and led to one of the worst experiences of my life filled with multiple forms of abuse. In retrospect, I knew from the moment I met him he would be bad news and I fell deep into it anyway. So you'd think when we actually broke up, I'd be happy, a release of negativity.

However, I wasn't happy and I was devastated for months. Due to the dynamic of the relationship, and the abrupt way it unfolded it was something that I actually had to work through for years and has forever changed multiple parts of my life. These kind of losses, the ones that actually are the most beneficial for you to let go of, can also be just as difficult to deal with and more challenging to actually see the good in it happening at all. It was something that came with some good though because it made me want to understand people better and more importantly, it ignited me on this journey. The whole experience even led me to writing about love and helping people shift their own perspectives. This book is a product of that.

The love that surrounded even a toxic relationship has transformed and fuelled the person I am today. I can see the loss of time, the hurt I endured, my loss of self, and the loss of a love I thought I had, all turned into the love I am building today. It all just shifts. I chose to let it shift and take the love from it.

I've experienced loss in many ways. Grandparents, uncles, relatives, previous pets, many who have had an impact on my life and I have love for. Every single one left me with an experience that has shifted my view on the world. Losing family, in particular, feels like you've lost a piece of your foundation, your home, and who you are as a person for family often has the biggest impact on your life. By family I don't just mean the traditional form (those related by blood or marriage), but I also mean friends who are like family to you. They all have that huge impact on shaping your everyday existence more than most.

When we lose these people the grief is the strongest, and so is the love. The opportunity to see where that loss has remained as love is easy to see in yourself, in the things you were taught, and in the ways that those people have shaped you. Those things are never lost after they are gone. I can remember even the smallest thing such as when I lost my first grandmother, I remember the joy I got when she made us soft boiled eggs with thin toast pieces to dip in. That love she created with this little breakfast joy stays with me today when I make quirky and fun meals for my husband.

I remember how my uncle would always be the first person to jump in with a hammer and build something for his kids and his nieces/nephews. While I missed having him in my life as I grew up, I later could see how the love transformed his kids, who are now four amazing people doing great things and who are genuinely nice people who treat their family well.

Our little Harvest was a true fighter to the end, but we made a decision from a place of love and respect to end her suffering. With the beautiful timing of the Universe I'm able to include her lessons right before submitting this book to print, further appreciating this chapter on love and loss. Knowing all that she taught our family, all the love we got from her and the times she made us smile will always pull us through her absence. While she passed away quite young at only three years old, I'm incredibly thankful for everything that she brought into my life and I know that I will never completely lose her. Of course it's incredibly important to mourn the loss in any dynamic and express the feelings that come along with it but knowing that there was more to it and you don't lose the love is incredibly healing.

It's good to remember in loss and many other things that while we may feel that things are happening to us, they are rarely about us. No matter how someone is lost in your life it's primarily due to something in their lives or even that things just no longer match up together in yours. The only thing that is about us is how we can choose to view and act upon what we are given. That is why we can choose to keep the love.

Everyone that has gone is not actually gone and that is the most important thing to see in love and loss. Love was created and it's never really gone even if it feels like it has. Choose to see it where it has transformed and choose to see the good in the challenges it made you face. It also helps me look ahead at those who I may lose in the near or distant future and know that I'll be ok. It's worth fully embracing the love that we have now without fear of losing it.

No matter how loss happens, the love never disappears. It transforms whatever is connected to it and that's where the pain lies. Let it change or remain in a memory and mourn the loss of the companionship, the feelings, the security - whatever it is about that relationship that made you feel that love. Know that the love still stays behind in some way and you never lose it. It comes back to you for the courage it took to release that pain and no longer let it affect your life. It becomes a formation of self-respect and love. Something that is beautiful in itself.

Does this change your perspective and make it easier for you to be open to love again after a loss?

....

Circle one: Yes   No

....

If you circled no, come back to this chapter after you've read the rest. Sometimes it takes a little time for a mindset shift to kick in. If you've circled yes, then give yourself a gold star!

6
Fear is Love

Earlier this year I was sitting in a seminar presented by Melissa Joy Jonsson, who is an incredibly smart and kind women who developed an energetic system that taps into the power of working from the heart. She mentioned one simple little phrase that stuck with me and helped me down the path of discovering what love now means to me. While our views on the topic of love are a little different, she mentioned "Love is just fear in disguise" and that was such a game changer for so many mindset shifts.

Diving further into the concept I learned that every fear you can think of can be shifted around into its love form. Some fears may be as fundamental as the fear of dying, which is the love of life, while others can take a little more thought to find the true love form. Even if it doesn't feel that way, it often can be paired up with a positive emotion and much easier to deal with the stress or anxiety around it. Even if it's still an unpleasant experience, it can be better tackled in its truer state.

I can think of many times when fear paralyzed me into not doing something that I wanted to. Even for this very book I had the fear of writing it, that I was going to be judged and that in the end I would have wished I hadn't put myself out there to write it. When I took a step back and realized that really it's just my love of expressing my truth and wanting people to think about things a little differently. Then I saw this was a book I really needed to write. Even the fear of judgement is a disguise for my love of wanting to be heard and respected. I can apply my own teachings and view this book from that love point of view. I realized that writing this book taught me even more things I needed to learn about myself and my own viewpoints. Therefore, a new love for myself and my perspective came forth, and instead of focusing on just the fear of being judged, I could see beyond it and cultivate a greater reason for writing.

Moving fears into their love counterparts is fairly simple and the first step. Once you figure those out then you can dive into the reason why the love is needed, wanted or just showing up for you. Let's try some examples:

"fear of being lonely" and turn it into what it usually resembles: "love of companionship"

"fear of trusting others"
is a "love of connection"

"fear of flying" is a "love of safety"

"fear of bears" is a
"love of not getting my face eaten"

Now you try a couple:

....

Fear of _____

is a love of _____

Fear of _____

is a love of _____

....

Look at you go! Turning those pesky fears into so
much love it's like singing Kumbaya around a
campfire with your closest friends.

Kuuummmbaaayaaa...

Now you may be thinking the love form may not
exactly feel like the same thing, but by flipping it
around you can see how it's very similar and now
you can choose to work within those parameters
with a positive vibe. It might not seem like a true
inversion of each other, but it will get you
moving in the right direction, towards more love.

Why is this so important? We all know thinking
positive is far more beneficial than negative so
choosing to take all the fears that have a negative
spin on you and morph them into the positive
perspective, you can then choose to deal with
what you truly want out of that fear. When we
focus on the fact that we have a love of
connection with others, we will focus on creating
connections that are meaningful, genuine and
eventually trustworthy, which was the fear we
had in the first place. If we choose to approach
relationships with the initial fear that others

can't be trusted, then we will just find untrustworthy people as we attract what we are most focused on. You get what you put out and by saying "I have a LOVE of companionship" instead of "I have a FEAR of being lonely" you will resonate on the vibe of companionship instead of loneliness.

Often we use fears as an excuse to avoid life and if we can use the universal power of love to uncover the majority of our fears, we may see that life is full of love instead of things to be afraid of.

We can also see that some of our fears are justifiable to keep as a warning because of the underlying love of something else that we have. For example, I will probably continue to fear spiders in the name of loving not getting webs in my hair or dying from some sort of random poison. A fear of bears will keep you from going up to them and giving Yogi a big hug and subsequently having him rip off your face, but it now means that you can treat those fears as warnings instead of something negative on your life.

Finally, when it comes to fear, I see that we have two options:

Fuck everything and run

OR

Face everything and relax

You get to choose whether it's something that makes you hide from the world, or embrace it because there is a more positive, love-based way to interpret it.

7

Hate is Love

**"The opposite of love is not hate,
it's indifference." - Elie Wiesel.**

I'm going to be honest and tell you that I first
heard that quote in the Lumineers song
"Stubborn Love" but after a little research
(thanks Google) Elie Wiesel has a bit earlier
credibility but it makes a lot of sense. The
opposite of love is just not caring and so is hate.

Think about anyone who hates something - if they really didn't care or it wasn't something they were interested in, then they would just be apathetic about it. So we bring in what hate is – a passion much like love, one might say two sides of the same coin. This concept has been in my mind and something I have known to be true basically since that song came out, but when we apply the same similar principles that we did with fear, those feelings of hate it can be recognized for what may be underneath it all.

Hate is not a word I use easily and even when it's directed at a person, often with time and effort it disappears. Hating a person in your life that still ignites that feeling is likely your reality at this time and understanding that the feeling actually comes from love can help take steps into letting it morph into forgiveness and letting go. Often, but not always, the people you hold on to that feeling for the longest with are the people you let into, or near, your circle of trust. Because you are close with them, they impact you the hardest since you've allowed them to be there. It's someone you want to feel love for, or they impact those you feel strong love towards and therefore the conflict between you may stir up that hate.

If it was just a random person on the street, the hate wouldn't really be there, it has to come from something that is of importance (love) in the first place. This is why hate within families is so common, we automatically have a strong bond of love in that circle even by regular standards, so when the conflict arises from someone who impacts that bond such, as an outsider coming in, it's harder to ignore and forgive. The hate still stems from your love of family. Hate stems (from) love.

While there are a few people who I've had feelings of hate towards over time, choosing forgiveness and ultimately love in the end has been far more beneficial. Even those who have deeply hurt you in this life, you can choose love in the end for their lessons and growth into who you are now, especially if you feel you've improved as a person. Usually that's in a form of forgiveness and when you let those feelings go, the hate goes with it and is replaced with why you felt the hate in the first place: love. The love for a relationship that went sour, a love for a connection you were hoping to have with someone and didn't, a love for a belief you have that felt threatened, a love for safety in your life and more. While this concept may feel challenging to follow for anything in your life you legitimately hate, look closer and you'll find an underlying message of love. If you can forgive, the hate goes too.

Only you can control if you hold on to hate or if you choose love and forgiveness instead.

Understanding the underlying message of where the hate comes from can be applied to everything, not just people. Maybe you just really hate mornings, when it may be that your body that just thrives and loves to be awake at night. However, taking a step back to flip around these labels of hate will help you realize what really bothers you. Sometimes legitimate feelings of hate, like you "hate" asparagus or "hate" mornings are really just things which you do not prefer.

The word hate has a strong energetic pull to it, so if you start to use it for the things you only really feel that way about, then you can uncover why you use it. Then take steps to forgive and find the love in every situation, including love for yourself in the form of letting it go. Get to that state of indifference instead, much like we do with love and loss, when we keep the love in the form of self-respecting love.

This message is all too common in topics of war. To quote from Star Wars: "We're going to win this war not by fighting what we hate, but saving what we love!" This is how all wars are started – love of money, politics, families, and power. While we use what we hate as a justification (people who are different from us or oppose us) to cover the motive of war, it ultimately boils down to protecting what we love. If the world were to focus on more of the truth of the love of what we want, we would take ownership and remove some of the hate we create. Then, operating from a place of love and honesty we may choose more peaceful solutions. You could probably agree that perhaps love wins far more than hate.

What is one thing that you hate, which you can now see is an expression of love:

I hate _____

when it's really love of _____

_____

8
Love is Trust

What comes to mind when you think of the word trust?

....

Trust is _____

_____

_____

....

Usually as soon as I hear the word trust I get a

vision of someone in a movie doing a trust fall as an ultimate trust exercise. It's often some sort of personal relationship and a pivotal point where the characters either trust or don't trust each other and causes a conflict or growth moment.

When someone says "I trust you" it's a great feeling! It's warm, it's fuzzy, and it has a level of ultimate positivity in it. Similarly, if you trust yourself, trust your faith, or even trust that your neighbour will take your trash out while you're on vacation, it all comes down to that similar feeling of having a positive connection about the situation. If we bring that into a connection of how love generally feels on the most basic level, it's the same and could be argued that trust is a form of love, especially as we are broadening out our perspectives of this beneficial vibe that surrounds us everywhere.

Now you may criticize this and say "I don't really love my neighbour" but don't you? Do you appreciate having someone to count on? Do you enjoy being in a neighbourhood that allows that kind of connection? There is a love towards that relationship if we can start to appreciate that love just might be a simple appreciation, positive interaction or something we value in our lives.

I know that trust in my own life is a huge compliment and I never want to take it for granted. I can think of a few people in my life who have instilled trust in me in areas that may not come easily to them. Everyday we are faced with people who may use us, information that needs to be secret but no longer is, or even having the honour of being trusted to provide information to people that seek it. A lot of my daily work is incredibly humbling that people trust my opinions on what they are facing in their lives. In fact, even if you take any of this book to heart and choose to implement some of the thoughts, it's a form of trust.

What if we treated the word trust as we did the word love (up until reading this book of course), would you trust easier or be more skeptical? Maybe you already treat the two on the same level – if you're someone who wears their heart on their sleeve perhaps you also easily trust everyone. If you're someone who's more guarded about their hearts within that society-built definition of love then your trust is also something that isn't easily given out. By bridging the gap between the two, seeing the similarities starts to build a feeling of love synchronistic to that of trust.

Build your connections of trust and you will instantly discover more love.

Now this one is for the critics. Your challenge comes when trust is broken. If trust and love are created together, then if someone breaks your trust or if you break your trust in yourself, does that mean the love disappears as well? No. In the same situation as when you meet someone new, you've never known them before and once you meet them and even if you never see them again you will still have met them. Any events that happen in your life are created and forever solidified in your existence and that is the same as another creation of a form of love.

When you use trust to create love, it's just another way of accessing it and if the trust were to disappear, you still have the existence of love. It's actually another way of having more faith in the trust you put out into the world. Even if trust were to be lost or broken, you've initiated that creation of love and it remains as it did when we discussed Love & Loss in a previous chapter.

Think about how you can start trusting more. If you're having trouble getting started, think about how it feels when someone trusts you. When does that occur? How do you think you can be a more trustworthy person? Working towards being a more trustworthy person and in return opening yourself up to trust others will just spread more love throughout your relationships and have a more positive flow.

Trust in love, as trust *is* love.

9
Love AND

All the things that we deem to be love in most of society is a form of what could be classified as Love AND [insert something else here]. Many of the things you wrote in the beginning of this book when you were defining love are possibly love with an additional factor or relationship dynamic.

When we think of love as the warm and fuzzy feeling in a relationship, that is often love with an array of additional factors. Love AND passion. Love AND connection. Love AND intimacy. The love for a child is love and protection, amazement, and even the need to care for another being that needs you.

If you were to no longer have one of these relationships or things, you are only losing everything after the "and." The love part still remains (it just will look and feel a little different than you are used to experiencing). The difference in feeling is just the removal of the supporting factors. It's like a hot dog, if you have a wiener and a bun with all the condiments — ketchup, relish, mustard, and mayo* — you call it a hot dog. If you had just a wiener and bun... it would still be a hot dog. Most of what we think is love is just the love condiments. Love is still the base of all of it, we just add stuff to it.

The best way to see some of the simplicity of the extras is to strip off the condiments in some examples:

Marriage Love - friendship, intimacy, sex, partnership, passion, dependency, travel partners, communication, mutual respect

Mentorship Love - guidance, knowledge, trust

Sibling Love - family dynamics, friendship, protection, upbringing

Career Love - fulfillment, life purpose, growth

Friendship Love - mutual interests, external fulfillment from primary partnership

Child Love - protection, legacy, sacrifice, empathy, encouragement

Self Love - respect, self care, self preservation, growth

Higher Power Love (Universe, God, etc) - trust, belief, hope, faith

These are just a few that come to mind and each one of these could have different dynamics. You can see that many of these things are not what most of us classify as Hollywood Love.

If you were to say you loved your boss or your mentor, in our society today you would probably get in trouble and would raise some red flags due to the nature of what love is universally labelled as. However, you can have love towards someone in a more platonic way when it's based on appreciation and a positive trust connection. You have love in what you get from that relationship. If we all moved towards this general understanding, we could see that those red flags would just be the extra things that may be inappropriate instead of the word love itself. Taking it off our radar as that taboo thing, the swear word so to speak.

Typically, the traditional views of love such as an intimate or sexual partnership, which is what

Hollywood likes to portray the most, will have more additions, things that are on top of the love or for our analogy's sake - more love condiments. You can also see if you were to end an important relationship and lose many of the additional pieces, you can still have the love that remains. It just doesn't have all the strings and you can let it go without feel like you've lost it all.

We often use the word love in more of a casual way when referring to things, rather than people. When thinking of this I get the visual in my mind of two young girls hanging out on a bed looking through magazines and one of them exclaims "I LOVE this shirt, it's my favourite colour" as she points it out to her friend. This is a love and a situation where it's love of something that evokes a positive reaction and excitement but the "and" is of style and fulfillment – whether it be emotional or something else.

While I think that people won't understand how to more casually say the word love to just anyone anytime soon, it's the concept behind it that's fitting and how easily we can actually share and receive love. Remember the 'and' in love situations and the word won't seem so hard to use, share, and grow among others. How nice would it be to say "I love you" to someone without having a bunch of strings attached? If it is a romantic partnership then it becomes something like "I love you and I want to be together", "I love you and I want to be in a committed relationship."

What are some examples like the ones above that you can think of? What is a form of love that you can identify and what are the condiments /extras when you take them off?

....

_____ Love has the extras of: _____

_____

....

Breaking down this process can help you put less weight on the love part of the dynamic. While it is the most influential and important, the weight of it often throws us into fear of using it. Instead, know that it's the extra condiments that actually define the relationship and the factors involved.

As I have learned from many of the people I respect (thanks for drilling it in, Universe), the "and" can also be used in situations where boundaries are needed while still expressing love. You'll notice that the word 'but' is not used much and that's because it basically deletes everything before it so there's no point of even reading it. When you say "I love you but..." you might as well not say I love you. By choosing to use "and", you can express the love and connection while still establishing boundaries.

I know that by swapping out this simple three letter word, my interpersonal relationships have improved drastically. I know in a few situations where I've had a quarrel with my partner, using the word "and" instead of "but" instantly takes on a new feeling. It says to him that I love him even though we are having this disagreement and he is doing things I don't particularly appreciate, instead of I would love him more if he didn't do those things, which is kind of how it is received.

Here's some examples of using "and" instead of "but" to enforce the initial part of the statement – the "I love you" - which is the part we're trying to enforce rather than delete. Try saying them out loud with using AND or BUT and see the difference in how it feels.

I love you AND you drive me crazy when you don't pick up your socks.

I love you AND when you cancel plans on me, it hurts my feelings.

I love you AND I need space from this relationship at this time.

I love you AND that last ice cream bar is mine so if you take it, I can't be responsible

for my actions.

We can see that it does not remove the overall care for the relationship. However, if you were to replace all the 'and' words with 'but', the feeling would be much different. It deletes love from the equation which is not our goal.

Seeing how many of our dynamics are love "and" something else can help use realize that love does not have to be deleted nor does it have to be the end all be all.

In case you were looking for some new hotdog condiment combinations, this is how I eat mine and it's delicious, in my opinion. If it's not your fancy, remember this is a book of no judgements. Which is why the next chapter is appropriate.

10
Love Without Condition

Unconditional love. Wikipedia defines it as follows: "Unconditional love is known as affection without any limitations, or love without conditions. This term is sometimes associated with other terms such as true altruism or complete love. Each area of expertise has a certain way of describing unconditional love, but most will agree that it is that type of love which has no bounds and is unchanging."

One of my favourite examples of unconditional love is that of a dog. My "first-born" dog, Farfel, absolutely loves me to the ends of the earth no matter what happens. I can leave her for hours when I go out or I can even miss her regular dinner time while I'm working a longer day and she still loves me without question. I could have taken her sister Harvest (who I introduced you to earlier) out for a walk without her and while she may be a little annoyed by being left out, but she will never hold that against me or love me any less. I love that little dog to the moon and back and even those who don't treat their animals as well, a dog still will likely be loyal and love their owner no matter what. There's no case of "I'll love you only if you feed me" or "I'll love you only if you give me belly rubs." Belly rubs are just extras and they love you without them. That to me really showcases unconditional love. There is love, period.

When I think of expressing unconditional love in my own way it spreads from both my personal and professional lives. From a professional point of view, I like to express unconditional love to people I work with in the sense that I send them love when I can as it's a very powerful energetic tool, especially as they are working with me. While that might be a condition in itself, I operate from the viewpoint that it doesn't matter what they are going through or the things they say. They will always find a source of compassion and love from me. Unconditional love in this sense is part of being a neutral point person for them, someone who will not judge (or at least aim not to) and be a safe place to speak their mind.

More commonly known, unconditional love shows up in relationships and it can be one the hardest dynamics to work with. It can be difficult to look at your partner and genuinely say "I love you with no conditions" when even though they are likely the person you do love the most.

Do you have deal breakers in your relationships?

Do you have things that you think "I'd love you more if..." Do you have times where you would walk away if something happened? Can you love someone exactly the same even if they don't agree with you? Whether you do or don't, knowing the difference between still loving that person for all the things you do and don't like, or withholding love because of it. Unconditional love says it does not matter what you do because I will still hold a place of love for you. I think unconditional love gets much easier as you expand your view on love and where you share it, because even if a situation or relationship changes or things are difficult, you can know that you can love someone regardless of what happens.

Unconditional love is best practiced by focusing on your most important relationships in your life and when you see any faults, anything that doesn't work for you to ultimately say – I still love you. Nothing will ever change that. It means not trying to change them, not trying to force them into doing anything they don't want to, and not telling yourself you'd love them more if they were different. Sometimes it even means that you don't question their returned love in order to showcase that you love them.

Unconditional love is the ultimate form of "I love you and...", instead of "I love you but..."

When in doubt, love like a dog!

11
Love for All, All Love for You

While I have a fairly strong (what I would refer to as a science-based) spirituality background, you won't find any love meditations or list of mantras in this book while you sage your space, although I do enjoy some of those things myself. If those things are beneficial to your practice of a greater connection to love and I would whole heartedly recommend it if it helps you. This book is more about the practicality within mindset and language to source more love. It's intended to be helpful for everyone, no judgements of your beliefs. See what I did there? Unconditional.

That being said, understanding that within spirituality and any sort of energy work there is a bit more of an understanding that we all are connected, we are all the Universe and the Universe is us.

There are countless stories that a wave of prayers or positive thoughts can impact other people. We know that it's not uncommon to be thinking about someone and they will call or text you even though you haven't heard from them in a while. We can often feel when someone is sad or mad even if they are expressionless. We get gut feelings about people or places that may be bad for us. We know that love is something we feel yet there's no physical evidence of its existence – at least that's easily viewed by the average person. These are all signs that we are all connected and if we are all connected then it's easy to see that we are what makes up the

Universe. Our infinite connections to everything.

If you function with the understanding that we are all connected, it's easy to access forms of love by sending it out. The more you love, the more you help others feel loved, the more you are helping the collective feel loved. If you are connected to all that, then you're strengthening love everywhere, including connecting back to yourself. Whether or not that seems like a farfetched idea, it's evident in people who give their time, money, vulnerability, compassion, anything they are able to give. You see that that they often feel fulfilled and loved in return. I know for myself, coaching and helping others brings me the most access to joy and love that I've ever felt. Even writing this book and hoping that others feel more love, helps me feel more loved myself because I am connected to all of you like you are to me.

Everything is an exchange of energy and when that is in balance, things are in harmony.

Knowing that we are all connected means we all need to give as much as we take, nothing more and nothing less. If we provide our time, we need to be compensated for it. If we donate our money, we are rewarded with the fulfillment of helping others or a cause close to our hearts. The reason why we sometimes feel lack of respect or lose our health is because we are giving way more than receiving, and while we may feel like we are getting the fulfillment from it because of the stories we tell ourselves, we often do it at our own expense. Giving when in balance with receiving helps us maintain our self-love, as it is respect for what we are needing as well. While I could write a whole book on energy exchange, for the sake of this one we just need to know to keep things in balance and know that if we are operating from a place of lack, you won't receive either.

Love works on a greater scale. Give love freely and it will come back to you, even if it's in a form you were not expecting. The more you send love to others, we are more likely to ask for it when we need it ourselves - and get it. When you feel like you don't have enough love, express it more. If you need some quick ideas of how to easily spread love, here are a few of my go-to's:

Send a text to someone you haven't talked to in a while. Whoever pops to mind first as they might need it most.

Take a few extra minutes to roll around on the floor with your dog (or kids).

Share your friend's small business with others.

Ask your partner what makes them feel loved and make an effort to do it.

Go for a walk to your favourite place for some self-care.

Leave a positive review at a

business you visited.

Smile at everyone you walk past.

Listen to someone who needs to talk.

When you're thinking of what is best for someone else when it comes to spreading love, one of my favourite examples is the book The 5 Love Languages by Gary Chapman. In the book there is a quiz to discover your love language.

It reminds me of when my husband and I were first dating and getting to know each other, and we did the quiz. If you haven't heard of this book before, I highly recommend checking it out and then doing the online quiz. It helps you identify all the ways that you personally like to receive love: Words of Affirmation, Acts of Service, Receiving Gifts, Quality Time, and Physical Touch. At the end of the survey you are given a score that correlates to your likely top preferences for receiving love. It brings some enlightening self-awareness and also the ability to share with your partner how it is that you like to receive love. It also dives into detail how this might be expressed with examples.

This book was very much a game changer in our own relationship because many times when we give love, we give it in the way we like to receive it, however other people may actually prefer it in other ways. To use my own relationship as an example, I am someone who sees Acts of Service as a huge sign of love from my husband which means that when he takes out the garbage or cleans up, it shows me that he cares about my time and comfort within our home. For him, he very much appreciates physical touch as a sign of love which means he's very cuddly and affectionate and if I express that to him, he feels very loved.

While that book is more aimed at romantic relationships and our more common perception of the love, it can be used as an example for spreading love to everyone in your life as well as knowing your strongest signs of love. If you haven't read the book, pay attention to when someone lights up the most and that may indicate how they prefer to receive love. Maybe your mother needs to hear I love you and I miss you, while your best friend might appreciate a small gift when you go traveling.

Anytime you come across ways of sharing more love, expand it into everyone – not just those who are closest to you. You'll find the universe likes to throw stuff back your way and those around you will start to reciprocate by your leading example. Start implementing more of these expressions of love everyday, then we will operate on a greater scale of more love for all, which means more love for you.

Now here's your homework: think of three things that you can do in the next week that spread love in a way that you may not have thought of being love before. Feel free to steal one of my examples.

....

1. _____

_____

2. _____

_____

3. _____

_____

....

12
Love Your Self

When I put out the question "what is self-love?" to some people I know, a general network of different backgrounds and ages, I got a variety of answers. With such a vague term that is vastly skewed by the ways of the internet, I wasn't surprised to read some of the replies ranging from describing a synonym of self-care to simple acts of pleasure. Self-love is a popular topic right now and probably the most important source of love. In a way you would think that it would be as easy as defining the very object keeping me sitting upright as I write this book - a chair.

Perhaps since many have such a variety in their answers to what self-love is, it's one of the reasons we struggle with it. We as humans like clear cut answers with clear cut solutions and with the concept of self-love being so important and lacking in our society, we grasp at anything to help us figure out how to obtain it.

But first, what is self-love to you?

Self Love is: _____

_____

_____

_____

_____

_____

Are you confident in your answer or does it feel

like it's missing something?

....

....

We all have our own perceptions and view of reality so we will experience everything differently, which is what makes living in this reality so exciting. So what we define as self-love, or anything we've discussed in this book, is different for everyone because everyone sees things through a different lens. What I hope is that the concepts and ideas in this book are opening up the possibility of what things could be to ultimately experience more love. More love is something you can never have too much of or we limit ourselves when what we think is self-love might not be and we are not fully accessing our potential for more love.

One of the biggest things that I saw when I asked the question about self-love, was that many people mentioned things I would consider as *self-care*. Self-love to them was taking care of their bodies, putting themselves first, and doing what makes them feel good. While self-care is definitely something that comes hand-in-hand with self-love, I would say they aren't the same thing.

You can get your nails done, cancel plans so you can get more rest, or make sure that your body is getting a proper diet - but it doesn't mean that you truly love yourself. If you do the act of self-care as a habit or even just because you know you need to but haven't developed the love for yourself overall, then they become disconnected. Continuous acts of self-care can help contribute to self-love but it's not the only factor.

Another perspective of self-love is being able to look at yourself in the mirror and have appreciation and love for the person looking back at you. Having love and compassion for who that person is in this very moment with no judgement. The strongest forms of love come without judgement and if you can truly say to yourself "I love you in this moment just as you are," is that self love? I would say so.

The downside to this is what if you get caught up in the stories you tell yourself and underneath you don't fully love that person who looks back? What if you show that person compassion and love and "say" that they are perfect the way they are but you're neglecting part of self-care to the point that it's not helping you love yourself. I think we so often tell ourselves that "I love who I am, so it doesn't matter if I'm 10lbs overweight" but the admission of the word "overweight" in itself is out of alignment in how we really feel. Too often the media tells us to just be who we are, in whatever lifestyle we want and still love ourselves but if we deny what we truly need to feel good and invoke that healthy self-care, it doesn't work.

One of the most impactful and books on life

clarity that I've read is the Four Agreements by Don Miguel Ruiz. One of the agreements is "be impeccable with your word" and this applies to yourself and others. I think it's incredibly impactful to remember that while we strive to be careful with what we say in order to not hurt others, it's equally important to remember to treat ourselves the same way. The hurtful things that you say to yourself, would you say them to someone else? Being impeccable with your word to yourself, is a huge and important part of self-love.

We may think we love ourselves but maybe we don't and instead we tell ourselves lies that we may not realize. I experienced this myself when I thought I loved myself because I was giving myself grace and time off to just be who I was in that moment, when in fact I was more unhealthy than I felt I need to be. I thought I had a really healthy mindset that I wasn't actually hating on my body or how I looked every time my husband took my photo. Personality wise, I felt I actually had finally come into who I am as a confident person.

Truth is tough, when push came to shove and I was presented with a stressful situation, I acted in ways that weren't a way someone with a strong self-love mindset would act. I faced the truth and realized that part of being confident in who I am is providing myself with what I need in all aspects and that includes choosing healthier options when I can and doing the things that give me what I need in mind, body, and spirit. Even though my mind was no longer hating on myself and I could see the beauty in the mirror, I was not actually treating myself in the way that was needed to feel good.

I need to be able to ask myself "am I doing the best I can?" and say yes even if the choices are not perfect. Before when I was thinking I thought I loved myself, the answer would have been no.

Part of self-love is knowing what you need and

when. This doesn't mean succumbing to an intense diet and fitness culture to look how you think you want. It means not forming habits that negatively impact you on either end of the spectrum. Feeling good about your choices and then being able to look in the mirror and say I love this person and all the choices they have made as well. Most importantly, knowing that when you say that, it's one hundred percent the truth. Self-care then becomes part of self-love but it isn't all of it.

We also have to consider self-love when it comes to external influences. The truth is, you are the one and only person you have to spend one hundred percent of your time with, so you need to make sure that person is taken care of and sometimes it means that you can't always do what you need for other people. This is evident in relationships, especially family relationships where our parents get old and we are told to take care of them, or even when people we know give us a list of things we "should" do because someone else says it's the right thing to do. However, there are times when you may need to step back and ask "is this best for me right now?" If it's a dynamic that causes you more pain than it helps everyone all around, then an act of self-love is to set boundaries. Even if your actions may affect other people but are necessary for your own health and life, it's required.

At the end of the day the only person who can hurt you is you and that goes for everyone else, so when they say that what you're doing is wrong, that's just a reflection of them and their own reality. It's something you can never control. You need to do you if it's required for your mental wellbeing. I know I've experienced this many times in my own relationships, knowing that making choices that are hard and can upset others and even myself, but provide me with the ability to be the healthiest version of me. It has been the highest form of self-love I can experience and I'm always rewarded in the end with the ability to be a better version of myself in turn benefit more people. Choosing you is self-love.

There is such a thing as swinging too far in one direction when it comes to all this self-love and care. As humans we don't really choose to live in balance as we are programmed to crave chaos, but when we are in an equal state we are the most successful. Knowing when we've gone too far when it comes to self-love is equally as important as not giving ourselves enough.

We need to look at the over use of self-care in our current society as well and how it can negatively impact self-love. Self-love is very much about being in alignment with yourself on all levels - mind, body, and spirit - and what you project inwardly and outwardly. Being confident in everything that you do and, to use the cliche phrase, "being able to sleep at night." Too much self-care can quickly transform selfish-care.

Selfish care is something I first wrote about

when I started my coaching business, I remember sitting on a ferry between Victoria and Vancouver in British Columbia and just bursting with ideas that I really wanted to get out into the world - frantically typing them out on my laptop so that I wouldn't lose my train of thought. One of my very first posts was that ah-ha moment of "well, I guess I'm not going to sugar coat any of my messages" and a true state of alignment. It was a simple post about self-care without being a dick.

The title alone pretty much summed up everything you needed to know about practicing self-care without expensing others. Like the hundreds of internet memes about cancelling plans if you're having a bad day, making sure to put yourself first, and always doing what you need are definitely important parts of maintaining balance for yourself and not falling off the deep end. However, it's gotten to the point where it's just an easy cop out for many and it's become too easy to cancel on a friend that might have really needed you or to create a pattern of easily avoiding life (fear) in the name of "self-care." This is where self-love and self-care get another disconnect.

We talked about self-love being in alignment with body, mind, and spirit so what if you are a person who loves to be there for people? What if your fears are stopping you from going out and getting the social interaction or exercise that you need in the name of providing yourself with self-care? What if your self-care actions cost a lot of money and that causes new problems? What if constantly saying no to things knocks you off your path because you're pushing into the uncomfortable spot that's not where you need to be. Then you're no longer honouring what you truly need. This is where we become cautious of using words like self-care in modern society, and need to get back to the root of what we really need in that moment, coming from a place of love. A place of love that is balanced between the needs of our own and the needs of others when we can provide it.

Most importantly, a place of love means spreading love. The fastest way to feel good about yourself is to make others feel good too. The more love you spread, the more love you get back. We forget that that when we claim self-care as a cop-out for meeting a friend, we may not see that our friend really needed us in that moment. That friend may feel let down and unloved because you didn't show up when they needed you, or feel a lack of connection and therefore impacting their self-love. Creating pain for others often causes pain in our own lives, and so sometimes the self-care that society claims is the best choice for us, actually knocks us out of how we want to be as people. How we have love for ourselves and being in integrity with who that is.

How do we know we are in integrity with ourselves? Integrity is defined as "the state of being whole and undivided" and that is almost perfectly synonymous with self-love. When we have undivided love for ourselves, we love ourselves exactly as we are and how we are treating ourselves. We embrace our flaws and have respect to improve them if we can. We talk to ourselves with kindness and without judgement. We don't take ourselves too seriously but we are serious enough to do what's right for ourselves. We know that being in integrity with oneself looks different for everyone because everyone has a different perspective of reality and the universe we live in. So, we know that being in integrity with ourselves means respecting our differences and loving it.

Then, you will see that self-love, when you fully embrace it, is the most important form of love. It's the love that is completely controlled by you and when you have love for yourself, you are never without love, even if you were unable to find it in any other way.

If you're not there yet, that's ok. There's so

much more love around us that can be found in everything and I would bet that even if you do not feel love towards yourself, you are still experiencing it in many ways. That is why we discuss self-love last, because so many people struggle with it and feel they just can't find that connection to love. Choose to respect yourself and fulfill your needs in all aspects of your life while choosing to spread love to others and you'll be in alignment and creating that self-love. Love for self.

Now let's try your definition again. Has it changed?

....

Self Love is: _____

_____

_____

_____
....

13

Love Wins

One of the most fascinating parts of writing this book is that I often sat down to write a chapter as I applied my own learned principles to myself in a situation. For that reason, this book has even taught me so much more about love and how changing my perspective on it has eased stress and provided clarity. From internal conflicts to my own relationships, to the ins and outs of losing one of my fur kids, to other friend/family

dynamics and professional interactions. We lead
and teach what we've experienced ourselves and
when I turn to those I value opinions from – they
have done the same thing.

The thing about love is the same as anything we
experience. We choose it. How many times have
you looked back on a situation of your own, or
even looked at someone else's life and seen how
their emotions and experiences are based on
their own choices? Whether it be an easy or
difficult path, we all have the ability to choose
how we feel and that's the hard truth sometimes.
We can choose to be miserable or we can choose
to be happy, just like we can choose to see love
anywhere we want.

Take a moment right now to start finding the
love in your life. Come back to this book when
you experience feelings of hate or fear to see if
there really is love underneath, or in moments
when you feel there just isn't enough love to go

around. There is more than enough love in this world, it's everywhere and if we take off our Hollywood rose-coloured glasses to embrace the possibility of expressing positively in the world, then it will be so much easier to feel and share. We can stop treating the word love as a swear word and use it without limitations or strings attached.

Do you feel like you have a different perspective on love now? If you think back to the beginning of this book when you wrote out what love meant to you, what would you say now?

....

Love, to me is: _____

_____

_____

_____

_____

_____

....

Has it changed at all? You'll notice that I never really defined love in a very specific way because love means something different to each of us, is whatever it needs to be for you, and can be found in everything when you look for it. Opening up your definition and removing constraints will automatically help you find more of love in your life in one way or another. That is the goal. Never have a day where you can't find love and keep track of how things change for you in your life.

And...for the analytical minds among us, here are some famous definitions of love. I draw some inspiration from these for my own interpretation of love and maybe you will too.

"What is love?
Love is the absence of judgement."
- Dalai Lama

"Love is like the wind, you can't see it but you can feel it." - Nicholas Sparks

"The path to love is our spiritual destiny."
- Deepak Chopra

"Love is cure. Love is power. Love is the magic of changes. Love is the mirror of divine beauty."
- Rumi

"How do you spell 'love'?" – Piglet
"You don't spell it. You feel it." – Pooh

"Love is the only sane and satisfactory answer to the problem of human existence."
- Erich Fromm

"Love is all you need and all you need is love"
- The Beatles

We all have the choice to look for the positives and choose the life we want to have while navigating the challenges that are thrown our way. We can let negativity overcome us or we can choose to live by the standards we set for ourselves. It's all around mindset, which when you shift it for a play on words – it's "mine to set." You get to choose how you think and what you believe. Choose to treat love as the magical, easily accessible thing that it is, rather than the swear word we cringe to use.

When you're in any situation and want to access the power of this positivity, the easiest of all things to believe in and my number one life rule:

Love Wins.

(because it's not a f♥cking swear word)

Thank You

♥

Ryan, the one I love most.

Farfel & Harvest for teaching me to love like a dog.

Amanda H., Amanda R. & Geoff for breaking the ice by being my draft readers and proof reading.

Ashley "WriterGal" Doan for final proof reading.
www.writergal.ca

Brian & James for helping me reconfigure my thought processes over the last few years.
www.bioenergeticbydesign.com | www.loewencoaching.com

Plus everyone else who has influenced my view of love and inspired this book.

Others mentioned in book:

Melissa Joy
www.melissajoy.com

5 Love Languages by Dr. Gary Chapman
www.5lovelanguages.com

Four Agreements by Don Miguel Ruiz
www.miguelruiz.com

Love Wins Essential Oil

Love Wins is a specially blended essential oil pure mix with the intention of connecting you to more sources of love. It's the perfect compliment to this book and I'd recommend you diffuse it while reading it to further integrate everything you've learned.

www.violetenergetics.com/store

Use Promo Code BOOKLOVE
for 5% off your order

"Love this product. It grounds me. I find it is best to keep me calm in situations that my anxiety runs high."

Manufactured by Amazon.ca
Bolton, ON

10399128R00070